The Girls in Grey

CAROLYN BOCK & HELEN HOPKINS

CURRENCY PRESS
The performing arts publisher

CURRENCY PLAYS

First published in 2012
by Currency Press Pty Ltd,
Gadigal Land, Suite 310, 46-56 Kippax Street, Surry Hills NSW 2010, Australia
enquiries@currency.com.au
www.currency.com.au

in association with The Shift Theatre.

Reprinted 2012 (twice), 2021, 2024.

NATIONAL LIBRARY OF AUSTRALIA CIP DATA

Author:	Bock, Carolyn.
Title:	The girls in grey / Carolyn Bock and Helen Hopkins
ISBN:	9780868199429 (pbk.)
Subjects:	Military nursing–Australia–Drama.
	World War, 1914–1918–Participation, Female–Drama.
	World War, 1914–1918–Medical care–Drama.
	Australian drama–21st century.
Other Authors / Contributors:	
	Hopkins, Helen.
Dewey Number:	A822.4

Typeset by Dean Nottle for Currency Press.
Cover design by Emma Vine.

Front cover shows (from left) Carolyn Bock, Olivia Connolly and Helen Hopkins.
(Photo: Nick Merrylees)

Currency Press acknowledges the Traditional Owners of the Country on which we live
and work. We pay our respects to all Aboriginal and Torres Strait Islander Elders, past
and present.

Contents

The Girls in Grey was first produced by The Shift Theatre in association with Theatre Works at Theatre Works, St Kilda, on 25 April 2012 with the following cast:

GRACE	Carolyn Bock
ELSIE	Olivia Connolly
ALICE	Helen Hopkins
SYD / HARRY / LEN / SOLDIER	Lee Mason

Director, Karen Martin
Lighting Design, Nick Merrylees
Sound Design, Nick van Cuylenburg
Set Design, Alexandra Hiller
Costume Design, Lyn Wilson
Stage Manager and Operator, Ben Leeks

An early draft of *The Girls in Grey* was performed as a work in development at La Mama Theatre in Carlton as part of the Explorations series in November 2010 and at The Shrine of Remembrance in Melbourne as part of Education Week in May 2011. Initial dramaturgy was by Jodi Gallagher.

CHARACTERS

Australian Army nurses:

    ALICE
    ELSIE
    GRACE

Others:

    SYD
    HARRY
    LEN
    SOLDIER

A cast of four sees the other roles all being played by the one actor.

SCENE ONE: SEED

The stage is in darkness. Lights fade up as letters begin to fall from the sky. A soundscape of tumbling dialogue gradually becomes audible… a letter to 'Dearest Lil', lines of the nurses' pledge, a journal entry, moments of dialogue from scenes that are not clearly audible. The three NURSES *become visible.*

ELSIE *and* SYD *dance together.*

GRACE *walks forward.*

As ALICE *gently catches a falling letter, folds it and places it close to her heart, the letters stop falling, lights change and the soundscape gradually becomes a busy port with a hint of a signature melody or sound that echoes later in the play.*

SCENE TWO: KYARRA

GRACE: [*as if continuing the initial letter to 'Dearest Lil'*] This is our chance. Really prove our worth.

ALICE: Independence! Out from under! Wild horses couldn't keep me away.

ELSIE: What a year it's been! My graduation, signing up, and a wedding! If he's there, I am there; it's as simple as that.

GRACE: They'll need someone of my experience. It makes perfect sense. Most of the girls will have three years; you couldn't sign up for the Reserve without three. I've got twenty. Got mine from Melbourne. And I'll not be confused with a Sister or a Staff Nurse, there's a big difference don't you know.

ALICE: I'll not be shying from this adventure! Passage to the rest of the world! After ten years I am ready for this. Really contribute.

GRACE: Make a difference. It's our moral duty.

ALICE: Not bad at all for a girl from the bush.

ELSIE: And it's natural, isn't it, to want to be there with our boys.

GRACE: My brother's there. Wherever there is!

ELSIE: Look at them! Some of the girls have turned up in hobble skirts!

GRACE: There she is.

Pause as they take in the ship.

The 'Kyarra'.

ALICE: White belly, green sash and the red cross!

The pace picks up again.

GRACE: Scribbling this quickly now as they have called us for boarding.

ALICE: The port is full, families, fiancés, children and the men.

ELSIE: Stirring aren't they, all together. And the wives. Holding on, willing a protective cloak about her man.

ALICE: Tears of farewell.

GRACE: You really should be here; they are flying our colours, Lil! Mauve streamers!

ALICE: Look at them, very spruce… barely a whisker!
Such pride.

GRACE: Nobody seems to know where we are landing, it's rumoured to be London. None of the lads know either! Will write as soon as I'm settled.

ALICE: Take it all in, who knows when we'll be back!

ELSIE: They say we'll be home by Christmas.

A ship's horn sounds and the cheering and farewells echo and grow.

Grace!

GRACE: Well, that's my cue.

ELSIE: Before they say you're too old!

GRACE: Wish us all Godspeed!

ALICE: God help us!

GRACE: Quite a boon! Red Cross have given us all a deckchair!

ALICE: Front row seats to the theatre of war, Matron!

GRACE: Give me a hand, girls.

ALICE: What have you in there?

GRACE: Supplies from the wellwishers. Mother wouldn't let me out of the house without three of everything.

The horn sounds again.

ELSIE: Here we go! Under the protection of the giant cross we sail!

ALICE: To serve King and Country!

ELSIE: Wave! They're waving!

ALICE: Where have they put the lads?

GRACE: Round on the other deck.

ELSIE: The rules. To protect us from our own folly… don't you know!

ALICE: Here's to us!

ELSIE: On our adventure!

GRACE: To Lucy Osbourne! The one who led the way! Without whom we
might all be confined to the walls of a convent.

ELSIE: Or drunken promiscuity!

ALICE: And… best be keeping the marriage quiet!

GRACE: I'll not be breathing a word.

ELSIE: If it is my fate, I can always join the Red Cross. Either way I will
not have him there alone! Till death do us part. To Syd!

ALICE, GRACE & ELSIE: [*together*] To Syd!

ALICE: And to all those bonnie lads, who leave as boys.

SCENE THREE: CAIRO

ALICE: Desert sands whip our skirts
What a sight we must be in all our sails!

ELSIE: But that morning star, makes up for it, doesn't it almost?
The long, long waits and the heaviness of heat,
Those magnificent dawn hues of pale gold and purple,
As the last strokes of night
Are painted out with light

ALICE: Is it a calm before the storm?

ELSIE: And look whose sandy eye we catch,
The sphinx
Under that brilliant turquoise sky
And the pyramids.

ALICE: The pyramids!

GRACE: There's a sight for your box brownie!

ALICE: Too true! On the count of three, ladies: one, two, three!

Pause as they hold a pose for a photograph.

GRACE: Look where we are!
Can you believe that we are here?
In this exotic place with its perfumes

ELSIE: Fortunes told in the sand

GRACE: The natives in splendid robes
Merchants peddling all sorts
Of wonderful

ALICE: The things of heady romance
  Promenades by moonlight
  With one of the gallant
ELSIE: That hasn't fallen for the wanton ones!
  They're at it tonight, the boys
GRACE: Our lot,
  Rowdy lot!
ELSIE: Can't blame 'em though
ALICE: Can't blame them for wanting to feel life before the whistle.
  Months of waiting
GRACE: They dance and sing and riot!
  In the hope
  Of recapturing
  Their lost and stolen youth,
  Some quench their desire
  In undesirable arms
  That condemn them to a long and uncomfortable convalescence.
  Outraged they are
  At being stung
  By the arms into which
  They themselves have flung!
ALICE: High tea at the Heliopolis Hotel
  With the 'who's who'.
  Palatial places,
  Silks and somethings
  Purchased at pretty prices
GRACE: And light duties, mostly tending the ill.
ELSIE: I wager we've sent the British girls into a bit of a spin
  With their scarlet capes worn only on senior shoulders.
ALICE: Here we are all turned out in red, every one!
GRACE: Running of the wards will require a careful negotiation.
ELSIE: Ohhh, Egypt!
  Quite the continental
  Trams *and* donkeys
  Motors and the camel.
ALICE: More tea?
  How about a show
  There's one playing now, don't you know.

ELSIE: Almost spoilt
   With all of this
GRACE: Doing all that a tourist would, we are.
   Tasting quail at the merchants' bazaar.
ALICE: And the minarets
   And that warble calling five times a day,
   We don't hear that at home.

SCENE FOUR: ALICE, HARRY AND THE SETTING OF THE SUN

ALICE: We don't see any of this at home.

   Pause as they take in the sunset together.

HARRY: What do you see, Sister Alice?
ALICE: Are we really at war?
   Are you really going?
   It's hard to believe
   Watching a sunset like this…
HARRY: I'll buy you a dress of that colour. An apricot spectacular.
ALICE: With the tuppence they are paying you!
HARRY: 'Ways to thwart a romantic moment', by Sister Alice.
ALICE: I will wear it! And I'll pluck a pink bloom from one of those enormous trees… for my hair.
HARRY: Ahhhhh! There she is! That's my girl! The one with the dinner plate stuck on her head! [*Blissful pause.*] I'll buy you a band of gold and put it on your left hand.
ALICE: Wait…
HARRY: I will.
ALICE: Is that a question? [*Pause. Playful*] Or syrup, sir? That rolls from the tongue of the soldier poised for battle?
HARRY: Never syrup, Sister, though I am, I confess, a *departing* sentimental!
ALICE: Oh, Harry, when?

   The reality of HARRY *leaving settles over them. The eyes tell all.*

   And so…
HARRY: And so… indeed. It won't be long now and the things we have always known will be forever changed, and in their place there will be things we have never seen nor heard before, some, the likes of which we will never see again…

ALICE: [*making it light again*] Kipling?
HARRY: Me!

>*She laughs. Pause.*

ALICE: This was lovely… Thank you.
HARRY: The pleasure is mine.
  May I call on you on tomorrow?
ALICE: I would like that.
  I am expected for dinner. Matron misses nothing.
  I will try.
  I'll leave a note.
  Same place.
HARRY: Under the second stair.
ALICE: Yes. And, Harry? [*Beat.*] I will!

>*They kiss.*

HARRY: [*gently*] That's my girl. Goodnight, then.
ALICE: Goodnight, Harry.
  Such a brief time, and yet… there it is.
  The great love.
  I am done for.

SCENE FIVE: GALLIPOLI

GRACE: The wind has turned
  There is a strange yellow sky
ELSIE: Anuket is angry, see how fast the Nile flows
ALICE: Sands whipping up a storm,
  Something is brewing
GRACE: The Light Horse
  Have tethered all the horses,
  They've been dismounted
  And are going to the Peninsula as infantry.
ALICE: Eight thousand steeds standing in the heat and the sun.
ELSIE: There is talk
GRACE: Something is amiss
ALICE: Something is not right
ELSIE: Rumours of a bloody blunder.
ALICE: Called to Luna Park, in Cairo. Complete with scenic railway.
  We'd never see this in St Kilda.

GRACE: We set fourteen hundred beds in four days.

ALICE: Heliopolis too. A swift transformation.

ELSIE: Grandeur gone
   Beds waiting in the marble lobby.

GRACE: Light by chandelier.

ELSIE: For so many?

GRACE: And then they start to come in
   The heavy ships,
   The 'Gascon', 'Sicilia', 'Itonus'
   Laden

ELSIE: With the hundreds

ALICE: Boat after boat

ELSIE: A nurse, one of ours
   Once here parading at the Temple of Isis,
   Now, pale with things she should never have known
   She talks of the shelling not ninety yards from the decks,
   As they pull the boys from the barges
   She talks of the red sea.

ALICE: Gone now are the charry grins
   Gone are the larrikins
   Who would woo and win

ELSIE: Here now,
   Is a throng of broken men.

GRACE: So many of them
   So few of us.

ELSIE: Are they starving, the walking ones?
   Queuing to ride the ghost train

GRACE: There is a rush for the food

ALICE: We stand by

ELSIE: We are shocked

GRACE: Bathe and bandage

ALICE & ELSIE: [*together*] Bathe and bandage

ELSIE: My soothing words belie my strangled throat. I think of Syd.

GRACE: Three nurses to five hundred men

ELSIE: There must be some mistake!

ALICE: Boys caked in sand, blood and lice

GRACE: Flyblown wounds fester in the suffocating heat

ELSIE: Makeshift beds crammed now into every corner

ALICE: Endless shifts
　　'Will you write and tell my girl?'
ELSIE: 'Will you write and tell me ma?'
SOLDIER: Will she marry me still, Sister, do you think…
　　Without me arm here, to hold her
　　Without one of me eyes?
ELSIE: She will marry you because you are still the lad that left
　　Because you love her still the same
ALICE: And if she doesn't then one of us will!
GRACE: One lad
　　Only sixteen
ELSIE: Looks at me with wide eyes
SOLDIER: So this is what it's like to die
GRACE: And even I,
　　With my steady hand and level head,
　　Move to take his hand
ALICE: Move to take his head,
　　Rest it in the crook of my arm
　　Like so,
ELSIE: I rock him
　　To his final sleep.
ALICE: No more musing of the heroes' welcome home.
GRACE: This is butchery
ELSIE: We are frantic for our friends
GRACE: And the train of wounded never ends.
SOLDIER: The Last Post begins to play, day after day after day after day.

SCENE SIX: BLOOD BATH

ALICE *enters, her back to us, and goes to the wash basin. She begins to wash. It is a familiar, practised and efficient ritual. She finishes and exits.* GRACE *enters and repeats the washing ritual, she is swift, efficient. She exits as* ELSIE *enters.* ELSIE *is a little disoriented and begins to wash distractedly.* ALICE *enters once more and moves to the basin.* ELSIE *has begun to scrub repetitiously on one spot… she scrubs and scrubs.* ALICE *suddenly grabs* ELSIE*'s wrist and completes the washing tenderly, catching her eyes… she holds…*

ALICE: Alright?

ELSIE: Yes, I'm alright.

> ELSIE *exits.* GRACE *re-enters and goes to the basin. As they continue washing:*

GRACE: Her lad was hit. I said she could go.

ALICE: Bringing him here?

GRACE: To Luna bloody Park.

> *Silence.*

Did you change the music?

ALICE: The little Irish lad

GRACE: Bless him

ALICE: Only so much trish-trash polka one can take.

GRACE: Anything from Harry?

> *They share a look.* ALICE *finishes then exits.*

SCENE SEVEN: ELSIE AND SYD

SYD *sits injured.*

ELSIE *enters. They share a long restrained look.*

She begins to slowly tend his injury. Her movements are assured.

ELSIE: Dear old soldier man… would you keep your head down in the future?

SYD: Yes, I will, Sister mine.

> *They share an intimate moment.*

Go on, no need to special me. There's lads that need it more.

> ELSIE *moves away reluctantly.*

ELSIE: I pause in the middle of spoonfeeding some soup to one of my patients when I catch a glimpse of movement outside the window.

I lean outside; the bright Egyptian sun shines on rows and rows of uniformed men. They look so smart, handsome and alive striding out with confidence to meet their fate.

Some of them see me up at the window and call out to me wanting to make sure I'll still be here when they return. They know they'll need me.

I smile broadly, reassure them that I will and wave them happily on their way.

Then I turn back.

SCENE EIGHT: LEMNOS

GRACE: Dearest Lil. Orders are through, we're moving. Shipping us to some island in the Aegean. Will write as soon as I settle. With love.

ALICE: As if the boys haven't been through enough… Hours on a ship, and now this.

ELSIE: Is there meant to be a hospital?

GRACE: Yes, 3rd Australian General.

This is the *right* beach.

ELSIE: And yet

GRACE: No hospital. No supplies. No equipment.

There is a delay in the Channel and the supply ship cannot get through.

ALICE: I can see the preparation for a landing, a clearing, but that's it.

ELSIE: What now? The boys cannot stay on this deck… four hundred arrive with the next… ship needs to turn around… We unload them…

ALICE: Onto the beach. Onto the bedrocks

GRACE: Landing with multiple gaping wounds, some without eyes, limbs missing, bleeding… Were any of mine amongst them… rather they be taken by a sniper bullet, than to suffer wounds like these that I am seeing.

ELSIE: What now?

GRACE: We do what we can.

ELSIE: Which is…

GRACE: We feed them, we pool our rations and theirs and make do… We dress their wounds with what we can muster.

ALICE: Our long undergarments have finally proven useful!

ELSIE: There is no water… the men are begging to be washed…

Bodies shattered… many are dying…

GRACE: And yet the boys say this is heaven!

ELSIE: Many die… lying in their blood-stained clothing. I can't tell you how futile it is. We have nothing to treat these men; we have only our words and our resolve.

GRACE: A colonel here declares that he expects half of them to die anyway and that we are too soft… There is no respect from some.

ALICE: Supplies slowly trickle down from other getups… The 2nd is fitted out beautifully… they give us what they can… everyone is pressed.

GRACE: No-one can deny the provisions for the wounded are absolutely inadequate. We are compromised. This side of things is unforgiveable.

ALICE: But no-one could have conceived… the Dardanelles

GRACE: And no-one will conceive of the neglect here until it is told

ELSIE: The devastation…

ALICE: No. No-one will.

GRACE: No-one could have…

ALICE: … conceived of…

ELSIE, ALICE & GRACE: [*together*] … any of this.

ELSIE: We have never seen wounds like this. I must not turn away now.
I hold their hands as I watch them cling, fade and disappear.

ALICE: Sometimes we operate without anaesthetic

ELSIE: Though you would never know. They are brave

GRACE: Help comes

ALICE: After a few days, yes. The orderlies are erecting tents around the boys… right where they lie… I do find it a little strange that while our boys lie on the ground, the prisoners are dressed in fresh pyjamas and have a mattress, well looked after… Is that how it has to be? [*Pause.*] War is a queer thing.

GRACE: Life has become a series of meetings and partings…

ELSIE: I know we make a difference.

ALICE: And we do.

GRACE: But do we? Enough though? If only people at home could know the worst of it… there is nothing they would not send. The censors are telling them that we are well-equipped.

ALICE: So the island becomes a sea of tents…

ELSIE: Row upon row, beach after beach of canvas on clay.

GRACE: Order slowly restored.
1 and 2 coming down with a dreadful thing.

ELSIE: 'Lemnitis' we dub it. Like a dysentery and flu. Something from the trenches? Men dropping like flies.

GRACE: 3rd stays clear.
This baffles said colonel.

ELSIE: Hygiene, sir. Drilled into us in our first year.

ALICE: And the 3rd is equipped with nurses.

ELSIE: The lice? The flies?

GRACE: Cut our hair. Cut their hair.

ALICE: Then the bitter winds.

GRACE: We wear the soldiers' coats.

ELSIE: And as they convalesce?

ALICE: They like to train us in basic infantry. In return for their healing. We learn to shoot.

ELSIE: Sporting.

ALICE: Yes.

GRACE: We had a battle to get here. Ranks would be fitting and timely too.

ALICE: Matrons made captains.

GRACE: So it will be. Like the Canadians. Our nurses made military.

ELSIE, ALICE & GRACE: [*together*] Thank you.

ALICE: [*play-acting as the colonel*] Would you consider a post as captain, Matron, back in a civilised hospital? You would be most welcomed in Alexandria.

GRACE: Thank you. But I will see it out here. My staff are excellent. Even the orderlies.

The lads are bricks. I would prefer to stay.

ALICE: Your service is invaluable. It shall be mentioned in dispatches. Good day, Captain.

GRACE: Good day, Colonel.

ELSIE: Thinking of you, Syd, on these exquisite days of clear blue skies. Airplanes circling!

Darting in and out of the sun.

ALICE: And you, Harry, where are you are in all of this?

GRACE: Dearest Lil. On the move again. The whole kit is moving. We farewelled most of the boys this morning. Some of them back home, some of them straight back in. This time I am certain it is France. Good riddance I say to the island! We all agree first stop will be a hairdresser! How I long for a cake of soap and some decent chocolate. I do hope there is time to take in the odd castle! Do write soon. G.

SCENE NINE: TWO NURSES DISCUSS A PATIENT

A hushed and private conversation.

GRACE: Has he moved?

ALICE: No, he's been just like that all day. Eaten nothing as well.
GRACE: Did he talk to you?
ALICE: Not a word. How long do we have to wait this time?
GRACE: Another month. This latest trial… it's a farce already, they know it.
ALICE: He'll be gone by then. Dress the wounds at the very least?
GRACE: Doctor's orders. Leave it be.
ALICE: He'll lose it then. The other too, soon after.
GRACE: Man-made medical experiment.
ALICE: He needs to sleep. I've given him something.
GRACE: Was it enough?

SCENE TEN: TIME OUT ON A LIGHT NIGHT

ELSIE *and* GRACE *appear huddled around a pathetic source of heat, trying to keep jolly and warm.*

ELSIE: If it's not the flies, it's the heat,
 Not the heat, it's the smell,
 Not the smell, it's the blood,
 Not the blood, it's the *food*
GRACE: If it's not the food, it's the damn cold!
ELSIE: Damn it to hell, it's so cold
GRACE: Look at me fingers… *freezing!*

          ALICE *enters.*

ALICE: And if that's not the worst… the water has decided to funk in the pipes!
ELSIE: What?
ALICE: The pipes are frozen solid
GRACE: Water famine
ALICE: Fire up the primus!
 We'll have to use the snow for the lads' cocoa.
 And how can you keep knitting!
ELSIE: Syd will have his socks.
GRACE: Seems the whole of Australia's been knitting up a storm.
ALICE: Battalion colours and all… well, very fancy!
ELSIE: Keep stuffing the stockings. The men will have their Christmas.
ALICE: Did the tobacco come through?
GRACE: Packet for each of them.

ALICE: And the beer?

GRACE: And stout. A bottle each.

ELSIE: Biscuits came through, and a gift each from Red Cross.

GRACE: Lavender scented handkerchiefs.

ALICE: Ooo… that'll please the boys no end!

ELSIE: Having their brows mopped with the scent of frilly knickers!

GRACE: Now, ladies!

ALICE: Mail's all sorted.

GRACE: Sssssshhh… quiet…

The sound of a distant drone.

Lights out!

ELSIE: Dropped a stitch!

GRACE: Quiet…

ALICE: No bell? Fritz! What are you up to on Christmas Eve?

They wait in darkness. Silence.

ELSIE: Not a lot, Alice…

GRACE: Hear it? [*Pause.*] The boys are singing.

SCENE ELEVEN: CHRISTMAS IN FRANCE

ALICE: December twenty-fifth. Against all expectations we manage to give our boys a marvellous Christmas. We nurses spend the day hanging red paper lanterns around the ward and hauling in a big pine Christmas tree. There's nothing like the smell of a pine tree to make it feel like Christmas. I remember helping Dad with the tree. Thanks to the Red Cross we are able to give our patients a dinner of turkey, ham, plum pudding, raisins, bon-bons and beer. To top it off there is jelly, cake and sweets. Every patient gets a little present too, which delights them, and some of them write home wanting to share it. As soon as they have their after-dinner smoke, they all lie down and sleep with a peace on their faces I've not seen before. As I watch their sleeping faces I think of one particular face and wish I could share just one minute of this day with him.

SCENE TWELVE: SACRED SUNDAY

GRACE: Dearest Lil. A red letter day for me with news from you. Today we've made it to church.

ELSIE: Here in the village,
> So pretty once, it would have been…

ALICE: Now rubble rules

GRACE: This little chapel defies gravity
> And stays standing!

ALICE: A little faith goes a long way

GRACE: It's good for the boys to get out and about…
> We chaperone the ones that can…

ELSIE: Quite separate from all the goings-on…
> Bit of respite!

ALICE: Breathe the air

GRACE: You've no idea how good it is to get a letter from home

ELSIE: A bit of commotion in the back…

> *Unseen by the* NURSES, HARRY *appears behind* ALICE.

HARRY: I think you'd better see to your ward, Sister

ALICE: [*not realising who it is*] Do you mind… [*She sees him.*] Oh my
> God, Harry!

HARRY: Blaspheming in church!

ALICE: You're here!

GRACE: Bit of decorum, Sister.

> ALICE *and* HARRY *move away.*

SCENE THIRTEEN: PICNIC

ALICE: How did you?… How long do you have?

HARRY: Forty-eight hours' leave! I've brought a picnic; let's not waste a
> minute… I've just the spot… It may not measure up to an Egyptian
> sky but French forests have a charm. What's left of them! I hope you
> like sardines.

ALICE: You know I do. Reminds me of a certain outing across the sands!

HARRY: With you, wobbling in a rather unladylike manner atop a camel…

ALICE: You managed to end up in the sand, whilst I, for all my wobbling,
> stayed aloft… I have the photograph as proof.

HARRY: That's my girl! Something for the grandchildren!

ALICE: I'll dine out on that for a lifetime!

HARRY: It'll get me through. Out there in the midst of all the mess, it's
> what I hold on to. [*He takes the photo out of his jacket.*] Funny thing…
> they carry them too out there, tokens of love, those they hold dearest.

ALICE: I found fifty-three German prisoners the other day, left for three days with no food or water, let alone any treatment. Forgotten. I'll never forget the sound of their cries. Thirteen were dead already. The nursing staff were dead beat, and some even reluctant to help, but a doctor rallied and we soon had them dressed and sorted… One showed me a photo of his sweetheart… another handed me a letter for his parents… and, despite all of this, I will see it sent.

HARRY *watches and listens intently.*

I kept thinking of you and how I'd want you to be looked after if…
HARRY: I never thought I'd envy a wounded man… [*Beat.*] Or a camel…
ALICE: Ahhhhhh… You've still got your spark!
HARRY: Tough as an old boot, is me!
ALICE: Not so old! Haggard and skinny perhaps…
HARRY: Nothing this day won't cure. Tuck in!
Here's to the work being done.
ALICE: Here, here!

Pause. *Inside the pause is the knowing of danger, the will and promise of love together, the fear of loss and the brave and stoic resolve to carry on.*

I don't want to ever let you go.
HARRY: Soon, Alice, you won't have to.

HARRY *exits.*

SCENE FOURTEEN: CONSCRIPTION

GRACE: The polls are in.
ELSIE: A nation divided.
GRACE: It's 'No'.
ALICE: They'll not be hounded to conscription, our lot.
GRACE: Rowdy lot!
ELSIE: Can't blame 'em though
ALICE: Can't blame them for wanting to sit tight and dodge the whistle
GRACE: They rally and riot
    On the banks of the Yarra
    While over here,
    Our lot are made fodder for someone else's cannon!
ELSIE: Call up all the young, strong boys and have them here now?

GRACE: I would have the men
    That have served,
    Time and time and time again
    Relieved!
    That is how I would have it.
ALICE: Even we women cast our ballots,
    Proud to have our say!
GRACE: There'll be no relief from the land we love.
ELSIE: Doing themselves proud though, the boys,
    They'd not have a cold-footer there
    Sharing a trench.
    Not when Fritz has his arms aimed,
    And if the shirker ran, they'd be the one to get it. *No!*
GRACE: Send them back into the fray
    Until Lady Luck grows weary of it.
ALICE: Would we have more bloodshed?
    After all that we have seen?
GRACE: I'll have no division here in my ward,
    No matter what the thought.
    We had a choice
ELSIE: We chose
ALICE: And we all are here.
GRACE: Then that's the end of it.

SCENE FIFTEEN: CASUALTY CLEARING STATION

ELSIE: Put in for a transfer. Takes a few weeks to come through.
ALICE: The RTO sending us down the line. I get sick of seeing the boys
    come in so smashed up.
GRACE: If we're closer to the Front we can do more.
ALICE: After nursing so many for so long… you want to be right in the
    thick of it with them… seems only fair.
ELSIE: Wanted a post at a Casualty Clearing Station.
GRACE: The closest we nurses can get to the front-line fighting.
ELSIE: Syd is supposed to be near there. So we front up. At first the RTO
    has little clue of where we're going exactly. Puts us in an ambulance,
    and we drive most of the night… really cold. Carrying only the bare
    essentials. The roads are ankle deep in mud, the traffic coming and
    coming, going and going

GRACE: Wagons, trucks, battalions of bedraggled men

ELSIE: Look at the lads! What they must be seeing.

ALICE: Still managing a smile, a smoke and a song!

The NURSES *laugh.*

ELSIE: They need a bath!

GRACE: And a damn good feed!

ALICE: Give them a wave, ladies!

Looks like they're our boys!

LEN: Hullo, Sisters! Hullo, Australia!

GRACE: God in heaven! Stop the truck!

ALICE: Grace!

GRACE: A needle in the hay! Stop the truck!

Len!

Lenny! Leonard Fisher!

LEN: Gracey?! Grace?!

ALICE: A minute, driver! Just a minute.

GRACE: Oh my God! Look at you!

LEN: And look at you! Alright?

GRACE: God, Len! Write to Mother… soon!

LEN: Where are you?…

GRACE: Down the line. Clearing Station. You?

LEN: The boys are almost done. Back in at dawn.

Some very important muddy place.

GRACE: Len, so glad… you'll be close…

LEN: I'll keep down, never you mind… we're looking out for each other.

ELSIE: Grace!

GRACE: Alright.

LEN: Alright, Sis.

GRACE: Matron, if you don't mind!

God bless you, Leonard Fisher.

ALICE: [*simultaneously*] Take good care, boys!

ELSIE: [*simultaneously*] 'Bye boys!

ELSIE: A breath

A minute

When all this war falls away

GRACE: Will we remember any of this?

ALICE: When we are scattered once again

ELSIE: How lonely we might all be,
   Without our Army family.

   The pace begins to build.

   Finally arrive, and it's so, so very different. The fighting feels on top
   of you, the sound… the wards.
GRACE: Tents all scattered and joined by these duckboards. Wooden,
   slatted things… so you don't sink. There are two roads… one for
   bringing them in and another for the evacuations…
ELSIE: No time to settle in, I'm sent into duty right away.
GRACE: Everything has been very quickly put together. Mostly stretchers
   on the ground. There are one or two bed wards, for the most collapsed.
   There is no flooring to speak of; not here anyway, the station was set
   up not three days ago.
ALICE: Electrics are on now. Yesterday they were operating by flares.
ELSIE: There's really not a lot of equipment and I am told to prepare
   for cases straight away. And then the boys start to come in. It's like
   nothing I've seen so far. The condition of the wounds is different.
   They arrive straight from the battlefield, with maybe a first dressing
   or a tourniquet on a limb that's hanging by sinew…
ALICE: Every man is just how he is from the trenches
ELSIE: Stone cold. Caked in mud. Each one needs to be undressed…
   which is difficult when the limbs are broken and the wounds are
   many… some of them so restless
GRACE: You see what needs to be done first… orderlies receive and we
   dress and classify, who can be immediately transferred, those that
   are to stay
ALICE: They come in; they go out… with a tag … like cattle. I catch their
   eyes once, twice… such gratitude at a drink, a kind word… and then
   they are gone… up the line.
GRACE: The abdominal wards
ALICE: Chest ward
ELSIE: Head ward
GRACE: The resus ward is for the ones who must wait for surgery…
   they are too collapsed…
ELSIE: The delirium of shock and unbearable pain…
GRACE: Many faces wearing the death mask… that stare you've come
   to know
ALICE: The shell madness

GRACE: Give pain relief and re-dress, give nourishment, and move quickly on, make sure that the instruments are continually sterilised and dressings at the ready.

GRACE, ALICE & ELSIE: [*together*] One after another after another after another.

ALICE: The theatres are continuous. Four here. Operating day and night. They do not stop.

ELSIE: I'm assisting surgeons now, in the theatres. Giving anaesthetics. Things unheard of back home…

ALICE: Amputating limbs, clearing multiple wounds, tying off vessels.

GRACE: Nobody talks, except to call for an instrument or such.

ELSIE: Gouging out shrapnel. Can't wait for up the line.

ALICE: The abdo wounds, most deceiving, they appear nothing and then the bowel will be found to be torn in six to twelve places… they'll never leave…

GRACE: Someone stop the slaughter.

ELSIE: The pressure lasts for a few days… relentless… we have to remind ourselves that there are meals to be had. A hurried break here and there.

GRACE: [*giving an order*] Prepare the sutures and splints for the next shift.

ALICE: Sixteen hours straight through, is suddenly normal. Then off duty. I've tended three hundred today. Aching back, exhausted.

GRACE: It starts to have its rhythm… and the constant guns could be mistaken for drums, you are loath to leave the men who so gallantly brave their broken bodies.

ELSIE: The moment you walk away someone goes, hundreds more are waiting.

ALICE: There are some costly mistakes. Many die. Yet not one complaint.

GRACE: Every patient's next of kin is taken with a message. Make sure all the names are correct.

ALICE: The saddest are the rows of men who lie unconscious… head wounds, and you hope they never know.

GRACE: How many are the walking wounded? Is that man carrying his Smith Dorian bag?

ELSIE: Have I missed someone, have I neglected this one or that? Was I quick enough?

The pace slows.

ALICE: And then that ward beyond

ELSIE: The moribund

ALICE: Where death is soon the cure

GRACE: The ones that have been put there,
    The men,
    The boys

ALICE: The choices we will have to make

GRACE: Too far gone

ELSIE: A throat, a neck,
    A chest in tatters

ALICE: And I,
    Am to make the waiting,
    the passing comfortable.

ELSIE: [*in disbelief*] Comfortable?

GRACE: Make them comfortable, Sister.

ELSIE: No time to find out who he is, what he dreams of,
    Who he loves.

>   *The pace quickens again.*

ALICE: I focus on this one, dispatch, then the next the next and next.

ELSIE: This man has his jaw shot away.

GRACE: Better ones to the less acute ward, this one to chest, this one to
    head.

ALICE: Brave hearts waiting to go to battle lend a hand.

GRACE: Wounded men becoming donors for the critical. A lifelong bond
    in the making. Transfusions on the floor.

ELSIE: Suddenly night.

GRACE: We are near a railway line. Line becomes a target.

ELSIE: We sisters ordered to the dugout!

SOLDIER: Lights out!

>   *The following is spoken simultaneously.*

ALICE: Shells start coming in. On top of us. Metal flying

ELSIE: Bombs start… tents shaking. Really close

GRACE: Theatre hit. Piercing the tents, heavy hail

ALICE: I fly
    Across the duckboards into the ward
    I won't be sitting with my head down with the patients out there alone
    Pitch black

Are you alright, boys?
I give them basins to cover their heads
Knocked off my feet
I'm falling, landing in something sticky
Scrambling through mud, feeling my way up
I sit it out under a bed with one of the boys.

The following is spoken simultaneously.

ALICE: Lights finding the foes
  Cranky Lizzie finds her mark
  Droning goes
ELSIE: Bells sound, sirens wail
  Hammer hammer of Funny Fanny Flanders
  Deafening roaring
GRACE: Time stands still
  Becomes the rhythm of the night when the battle is on and The Push
  starts.
GRACE: Head count! At night though, they are too close, I hardly notice.

SCENE SIXTEEN: SHELLSHOCK

GRACE: Too soft?
  Too soft!?
  The flesh I see is too soft!
  Were it made from the stuff that tore it,
  The man would be a shield
  And this bloody war won yesterday!
  My head. I cannot see clearly.
  Are the lamps up?
  I have wet myself.
  Any loud noise, any fright.
  I am shaking.
  My head is pounding.
  I go on.
  I go on
  But in the eyes
  Of all the shell-shocked men,
  I see myself.
ALICE: Alright?

GRACE: No, I am not quite right.
    I am as they are
    Half crazed and raving
    In fear.
    Suspended in this moment
    I am stuck in the eye of it.

      Silence.

SCENE SEVENTEEN: THE GAS

ALICE: Beware the scent
    They say,
    Of the pepper
    And the pineapple
ELSIE: Or on another day,
    The smell of mouldy hay
ALICE: That finds the eyes
GRACE: The throat
ELSIE: And then the lungs
GRACE: Turns to acid on the skin
ALICE, GRACE & ELSIE: [*together*] Beware the touch.
GRACE: Beware the blistering.
SOLDIER: And then,
    Again,
    This time clinging to the clothes,
    Clinging to the bayonets, the mud,
    A single cylinder
    Sliding a quiet path
    Along the bottom of the trenches,
    All are changed then,
    Covered
    In a grey-green film.
    All turned a strange sepia.
ALICE: This sinister snake
    This extermination.
GRACE: From where did such a hatred spring?
    That one would rid the other out,
    Like vermin?

ELSIE: What it does to a man's skin.

 What it must be doing to the life within?

ALICE: Wards reversed…

 Heads to centre

 Cocaine to the tortured eyes

GRACE: Roll up the walls… let in the air!

ELSIE: Whole wards rocked

 With the gasping

ALICE: Roll up the walls!

 Let in the air!

GRACE: Nurses, *beware!*

 Never too close without a monster mask

ELSIE: Lest we choke too…

ALICE: … on the poisonous residue.

SCENE EIGHTEEN: LETTERS TO MOTHERS

/ denotes where the next line starts.

GRACE: Dear Mrs Draper

ALICE: I regret to inform you/ of your brother's death. He died of his wounds

ELSIE: Dear Mr and Mrs West

GRACE: I had the privilege of nursing/ your son and it is my sad duty to inform you of his death

ALICE: Dear Mrs Macpherson

ELSIE: I am very sorry to inform you/ of your husband's death. He collapsed this morning

GRACE: I was with him when he died

ALICE: I was with him when he died

ELSIE: I was by his side

GRACE: Dear Miss Shepherd

ALICE: I wanted you to know his last thoughts/ were of his family

ELSIE: Dear Mrs Alexander

GRACE: He was very grateful for everything I did/ although we could do very little

ALICE: Dear Mr and Mrs Skinner

ELSIE: Even though his injuries were severe/ he never complained

GRACE: Dear Miss Calvert

ALICE: The bravery of your fiancé/ was inspiring, but despite a valiant effort he was unable to rally

ELSIE: I am so sorry for your loss

GRACE: I am so sorry for your loss

ALICE: I am so sorry for your loss

GRACE: Dearest Lil. Got your news. Good for you. We are in the thick of it here. If you are thinking of coming over… don't, it's too… But when you see the boys at home, and you will because they're missing things, treat them with the very best, 'cause they have been to hell.

SCENE NINETEEN: SOMETIMES IT GETS LIKE THAT

ALICE: Orders come to move.

ELSIE: And so, where the boys are, we nurses go

ALICE: In three days… the hospital is gone… Patients are evacuated…

ELSIE: Taken up on anything that moves

ALICE: Soon there is no trace of the coming and the going… off with a cheer

GRACE: Eyes ahead to the new site As we travel long into the night

ALICE: Plan the camp and pitch here.

GRACE: Be prepared to receive two thousand.

ALICE: Sometimes it gets like that Like thousands of them Calling you at once

ELSIE: Of course you do your best Worst are first

GRACE: And sometimes everything goes quiet.

   Silence.

ALICE, ELSIE & GRACE: [*together*] And we all listen And we wait

ALICE: For that drone

ELSIE: That whistling

GRACE: And then the thud

ELSIE: And you wonder
GRACE: Where it fell
ALICE: And who it got.

SCENE TWENTY: ANNIVERSARY

ALICE, ELSIE, GRACE & SYD: [*simultaneously*] Leave!
ALICE: It is hard to leave the others to it.
ELSIE: Oh, leave at last! Meeting you across the Channel, with a chaperone
    of planes!
SYD: Six months is too bloody long, isn't it?
ELSIE: Playing for a minute, in our thatched farmhouse
SYD: Husband and wife
ELSIE: Cycling to Brighton and on to Bath…
SYD: Drinking in that green!
    Those cathedrals and sights
ELSIE: Walking you to the barracks
SYD: By the fire at night,
    Dinners in.
ELSIE: Is this what it feels like?
SYD: It'll be like this, when we are home, love
ELSIE: This quiet. You and me.
SYD: Not even the occasional Zeppelin!
ELSIE: Thank heavens for the far, far away!
SYD: Happy anniversary, heart.
ELSIE: Happy third.
    The next, God willing,
    In our sun-kissed home.

    She moves away.

How is it
That in such a short time
I can melt and hope for the future
It seems so close
And yet
I forget
For a moment
In a breath,
In a blink it can be taken away.

I travel now
Away from it…
All too quickly reminded
How can we dream a life beyond this kind of living?
I stop in at Notre Dame
And light a candle
I force my faith
I lock my prayers in an iron-clad will.
I take the key
And cast it deep into myself.
I dry my eyes
And breathe the air.
I call myself again, to do my duty.
And trust the work of my able hands
We are side by side,
We will see it out.
I know it.

SCENE TWENTY-ONE: THINGS BETTER LEFT UNSAID

The NURSES *are huddled in a bunker.*

ELSIE: Here, have a nip, courtesy of the colonel.

ALICE: To calm our nerves

GRACE: Better late than never!

ALICE: Do you write everything in that diary?

GRACE: My way of keeping an inventory of things…
Of all the little things I might not remember if I wait until morning.

ALICE: If we are still here!

GRACE: For memory. Mine and theirs.

ELSIE: I write of the sights and the wonders we are seeing… the way the light plays on the river at night

GRACE: One still manages to have a picnic

ALICE: Of the days that will see us forever changed…

ELSIE: What we cannot write in letters home.

GRACE: That is true

ALICE: So, this is how she would spend her days, they'll say…

GRACE: Days spent in the barking of orders and washing of wounds, and the details of the coming and the going.

ALICE: The infernal bugle!

GRACE: And her nights spent in thought…

ELSIE: She dreams of voices that weave their way to her pen

GRACE: She talks of all her suitors… this one and that, until one particularly takes her fancy and leaves all the rest in their wake.

ALICE: Into the diary she fondly calls: 'My silent hands'

GRACE: The hands that saw the scalpel!

ALICE: 'My, Sister, you are certainly the A to Z of nursing'

ELSIE: Little anecdotes, on the return home, become quite the talk at dinner parties…

GRACE: Maimed men made medical miracles!

ALICE: Goodness! All that mud! How did you cope!

GRACE: What moments she cares to share become curiosities for those who want to know… 'What was it like, really?'

>   *Pause.*

ALICE: Some things are better left right here.

GRACE: The horror is better left.

>   *Pause.*

ALICE: Home. I fear it will have grown particularly tame in comparison.

>   *The sound of a massive explosion.*

SCENE TWENTY-TWO: FROM BATTLE TO BED AND BEYOND

SOLDIER: Heavy dull feeling
Know something's up.
Sky, ground, sky
Rain, mud, then
Nothing
Waiting,
Really quiet, then
Guns, rain, pain, guns
Nothing
Dragging, then
Pat's missing
Where's Pat?
Nothing
Day, night, day

Lie in it
Smells.
Things smell.
Notice there aren't any birds
Can't hear anyone.
Then running
Yelling running
Fire! Noise!
Fire noises blasting
Dragging
Nearly there, mate… hang on…
Pat?
Someone next to me.
Near my face
Pat.
Pat is
Not moving. Can't move
God, no eyes
Pat's face
Out
Wounds reeking with the stale of waiting
Already too long.
With a will willing out the waiting
In and out of seeing,
Then in and out of feeling
Arms lifting
All light
Out
Being carried,
Hurried voices
Pat's voice?
Barking orders
Body pulled and peeling pain
Pressure and pincer pain
Bloody cold smiling
Sounds of music somewhere
Out, in, out,
Blinding pain

Out
Nothing
Knowing hands, clever and quick
Cutting, while carried

SCENE TWENTY-THREE: PERMISSION

The NURSES *deliver the following in hushed tones.*

NURSES: This one,
     This second stretches
SOLDIER: Cool morphia
NURSES: I am about to cross the line
     Beyond my jurisdiction
SOLDIER: Cool sweet conscious fading
NURSES: The doctor's role
     All others occupied
SOLDIER: Music is the Siren's song
NURSES: Knowing what to do
ELSIE: Know this
     Seen them do it
     Know how.
     I can
SOLDIER: Out then.
GRACE: Clean it, dress it, move on
NURSES: Cannot.
SOLDIER: Hollow voices echo loud
NURSES: Cannot move on
     Waste of life
     Waste of a man
     Will not wait.
SOLDIER: Out
NURSES: Will
     Not wait
     I can
     Can save him.
     Save others
     Do more
     Do it now.

Can save this man here and now.
Others occupied.
Cross the line.
I save.
SOLDIER: Eyes flicker
NURSES: I can
SOLDIER: Lights on
NURSES: I have.
SOLDIER: Very bright
ALICE: Catch eyes… they hold…

> *Beat.*

NURSES: Cross the line.
I save.
SOLDIER: Face of an angel
Gentle words
Firm hand
ALICE: Lie back, soldier
GRACE: Lie back, lad
Be still
ELSIE: Something for the pain
SOLDIER: Where?
ELSIE: At a Clearing Station
GRACE: Moving you … now
Hold him
SOLDIER: Where's Pat?
ELSIE: In France, in Fromelles.
GRACE: You are wounded
ALICE: You were lucky… some not so
GRACE: The whole of the 5th.

> GRACE *and* ALICE *catch eyes—this is Harry's battalion.*

I am sorry, I can't tell you any more.
ELSIE: Lie back, soldier,
Be still
SOLDIER: Smell. Putrid smell
ALICE: No other choice…
GRACE: Gas, gangrene
You would have died

SOLDIER: Very lucky?
　　Pat?
ELSIE: You'll make it, lad, be strong.
　　Something to help you sleep.
ALICE: Sleep
GRACE: sleep
ELSIE: Deep sleep
SOLDIER: First sleep without legs
ELSIE: He says
　　Slipping under and away and beyond
GRACE: Gibson
　　James
ALICE: Harry?
ELSIE: And brother
　　Patrick.
　　Pat.

SCENE TWENTY-FOUR: HARRY'S LETTER

HARRY: My dearest love. I'm snatching some time to write a little note
　　to you. We are right in the middle of it all and as soon as I am able to
　　rest for a moment it seems I am needed again. I miss you terribly. If
　　I could just have you with me for one moment, how happy I would
　　be. The country around us is in ruins but springing up in the cracks
　　and holes are red poppies and blue cornflowers. Little reminders of
　　how life used to be. Think of me, my darling, and remember me in
　　your dreams. Always yours. Harry.

SCENE TWENTY-FIVE: ODE TO HARRY

ELSIE: Here it is an endless winter.
　　Lying, the countless,
　　Under blankets of mud.
　　Flesh torn from limbs,
　　Limbs gone.
　　Faces gone.
　　Eyes gone.
　　Love gone.
ALICE: Buried where he fell.

GRACE: Buried where they fall
ELSIE: The father
ALICE: The lover
GRACE: The brother
ELSIE: The son.
ALICE: All silent.
    Words gone.
    Laughter gone.
GRACE: We too
    Could build a chapel of bones
    In memoriam
    Like St John.
    Pay homage to the warriors.
    Right there, on the Somme.
    On those fields where
    Now the poppies
    Bloom in a crueller shrine.
ALICE: And will the poppies bloom on that spot where Harry fell?
    Will his marrow nourish that stone?
    Is his blood now the nectar?
    Are the blooms deeper
    In hue
    For his love lost?
    Show me his bones.
    His battered self.
    That I can believe his death.
    Give me back something of
    Him
    That I may have my own shrine.
    I am not content with this memory of him.
    Will not be consoled
    With this box of trinkets.
    You give me back his uniform?
    Where is his face?
    You give me back his rank and file
    Where is his face?!
    Where are those brave arms?
    What have you done with them?

What have you done with him?
Let me crawl into his damp skin
Still chilled
Underneath that field.
Bury me alive with his bones.
That I may give him back
Life.
Let me breathe for two.
And when we are one,
Cover us up.
Cover us both up.
Cover all of us up,
And mark it there.
On that spot.

ALICE, GRACE & ELSIE: [*together*] Lest we forget.

ALICE: He took me with him today.

Every soldier's sleep
Lies multiplied.

GRACE: We are stuck in a heavy web.

Us all.
See us *all* in the fields.
And have all the poppies bloom
Where so many fell and fall.
And let it be known as the
Chapel of Blood.

> *Silence.*

> *In a ritual for the fallen, the* NURSES *move across the stage in unison, placing poppies until there are rows and rows at perfect intervals on the floor.*

SCENE TWENTY-SIX: SOME OF US WILL STAY

ELSIE: Whispers of a treaty

GRACE: I have a tightness in my chest.

ELSIE: Months ago

We'd never have thought it
News of Syd and our reunion.

GRACE: Terrific cough
   Body aches
   Fever, clammy, chills.
ELSIE: The streets now lined
   With banners and flags
GRACE: Night sweats
   Like the men.
ELSIE: All dancing, songs of victory
   At last!
   Our Armistice
GRACE: Too quiet now the guns have gone
ALICE: She is wearing the death mask.
GRACE: Dearest Lil. They say that this one is from Spain, and it's a damn
   dog of a thing! Haven't been able to shake it. Doubt I'll be home,
   love. You must not fret, my dearest friend. I will be at rest in such
   fine company. Perhaps one day you will pay me a visit. All my love.
   Grace.

   They bathe me and dress me in my grey uniform, apron and cape,
   starched and lovely. My coffin draped with our flag and my cap and
   belt on top.

   They take me on a wagon up the slope toward the little chapel.

   Behind it, the military cemetery: rows and rows of graves dug into the
   hillside. Here I will always have a view of the castle. I'll be watched
   over by the mountains.
ELSIE: Here somewhere they say her brother is buried. Taken by that
   sniper. May they find each other.
ALICE: What a send-off... the firing party, officers, the lads, orderlies and
   ourselves.
ELSIE & ALICE: [*together*] We wish you Godspeed.

      ELSIE *and* ALICE *leave* GRACE *on her own.*

ELSIE: Orders are through, we're moving!
ALICE: So many friends, once thrown together,
   Now loath to leave
ELSIE: Look at the lads...
   Bottomless thirst...
   Faces beaming!

ALICE: I'll not travel too far though, not yet

ELSIE: Long goodbyes… the splitting up
  The long passage home
  Oh, Syd!
  Us and home at last!

ALICE: And you, Harry, amongst it somewhere. Out there.
  This peace is bittersweet.
  Holding you closer still
  With a promise, I'll not forget
  Your face
  Your arms
  At every sunset.

  Pause. The nurses recite The Pledge of Service.

  I pledge myself loyally to serve my King and Country and to maintain the honour and efficiency of the Australian Army Nursing Service.

  ELSIE *joins in.*

ALICE & ELSIE: [*together*] I will do all in my power to alleviate the suffering of the sick and wounded, sparing no effort to bring them comfort of body and peace of mind.

  GRACE *joins in.*

ALICE, ELSIE & GRACE: [*together*] I will work in unity and comradeship with my fellow nurses. I will be ready to give assistance to those in need of my help, and will abstain from any action which may bring sorrow and suffering to others. At all times I will endeavour to uphold the highest traditions of Womanhood and of the profession of which I am part.

  The NURSES *stand together as the lights fade to black.*

THE END